For The

P.J. Cartwright

India | USA | UK

Presentation by *BookLeaf Publishing*

Web: www.bookleafpub.com

E-mail: info@bookleafpub.com

ISBN: 9789358316384

First edition 2023

For the stars in my sky.

ACKNOWLEDGEMENT

A huge thank you to everyone who has ever supported my writing and encouraged my book buying habit.

PREFACE

For the storms that rage
inside and out, keep going,
you will find your peace.

Storms

There is nothing like the feel of a storm.
The sky darkens so fast.
You can feel the electricity in the air,
the pressure building,
the sudden calm before the wind starts
a gentle breeze that starts to pick up.
A few drops of rain the only warning you get
before the heavens open
and its like the gods themselves are weeping.
The rain is thrashing down,
the wind is howling, raging,
pulling at centuries old oak,
threatening to tear it from the ground.
The dark sky is lit up,
a fork ripping through the black
and you count the seconds until,
you can feel the rumble of the thunder
in your bones and in your stomach.
The lightning gets brighter,
the rumble louder,
you could swear you almost feel the earth move
as its right on top of you.
And when it passes
for a moment the world is quiet,
and still.

The smell of the earth is refreshed
and the colours in the world are brighter,
and you feel lighter.

Mother Says

The are things in the shadows,
my mother would say.
Be careful of the shadows,
lest they take you away.

Beware what hides in the darkness,
my mother would tell.
For the things that hide in darkness,
are looking for a soul to sell.

Stay inside at midnight,
my mother would warn.
For if you're caught at midnight,
all we can do is mourn.

Stay away from spirits,
my mother would yell.
Those taken by the spirits,
are taken straight to hell.

Never trust the shadows,
my mother would cry.
But now I find the shadows,
to be a comfort as I die.

I Dream Of You

You were in my dreams last night,
my subconscious reminder of how I miss you.
You're always gone with the morning light.

A half-remembered smile in soft firelight,
I could drown in eyes that blue,
you were in my dreams last night.

Kissing my hair, whispering goodnight
as I trace the lines of your tattoos,
you're always gone with the morning light.

In my life, you were always the light,
I used to live and breathe you.
You were in my dreams last night.

I should've paid attention, things didn't feel
right.
Now I know, I could never trust you,
you're always gone with the morning light.

Without you part of my heart has died,
it tears me apart how badly I miss you.
You were in my dreams last night,
but you're always gone with the morning light.

I'd Do It Again

Those nights we spent together, drinking
whiskey just because.
Talking and laughing with your record player on.
The inside jokes, shorthand codes just for us,
it all feels like a half forgotten song.

We'd watch black and white movies lying in
your bed.
It felt like no one could know me like you,
you'd show me all the things going on inside
your head.
All I ever wanted was to stay beside you.

Sometimes when I'm caught in the heaviest of
rain,
I remember how hard we used to fight,
hurling words we didn't mean just to cause a
little pain,
screaming in the street in the middle of the night

I think about you sometimes, and for months and
years
I compared everyone else to how you made me
feel.
But the hours I cried over you, all of the tears,

it wasn't worth how long it took my heart to
heal.

I understand we were too toxic and too volatile
I know we're better apart, I'm not that naïve
and though I hated to admit it, it took me a while
I think the best thing you did for both of us was
leave.

I still don't regret the time we were together,
and if I'm honest with myself I would probably
choose,
even though I know we wouldn't be forever;
I'd still do it all over again with you.

Without You

Without you the days run into each other,
endless and bleak. There is nothing to break up
the greyness and the sadness. Colours are muted.
Lifeless and dull.
I find no joy in anything.

Without you I find myself starting to notice the
passage of time again. The days may change but
the emptiness remains.
I find no joy in anything.

Without you I start to remember that the days
were not always good. When we fought, and you
made me miserable, and cry again and again.
The rose tint may be wearing off, but still.
I find little joy in anything.

Without you I find I have anger in place of
sadness. There is a warmth where there was
cold.
The sun is shining and I do not feel empty, as I
soak up the rays of happiness from those around
me.
I am finding joy in little things

Without you I have learned from my mistakes.
The memories of you will fade and my heart will
heal. I will not let you damage me and keep me
from happiness. You will not be my great lost
love, just another boy in another song.
I will find joy in something.

Without you I have taught myself to stand up on
my own. I know what I need now, and what I
want from this life. You were not it, but I have
found it in him, and without you, I would not
have.
Now I find joy in everything.

Murder At The Masquerade

I stand here in this exquisite hall,
surrounded by those hiding who they are.
The perfect cover, this masquerade ball,
no one knows who I am so far.

I stand in a corner in my beautiful dress,
you thankfully do not recognise me.
How could you, when you left I was a mess
and this isn't where you expect me to be.

You think I am home, in bed with the flu,
you could barely contain your glee.
When I said I would not be attending with you,
you barely gave a second thought to me.

As soon as you left I put on a gown-
the one that nobody saw me buy.
I put on my mask and followed you down,
to the place you would unfortunately die

I watch you now as you dance and sing,
clearly having the time of your life.
The woman you're with, is she the new fling?
How fast you've forgotten your beloved wife.

The knife is cold against my palm,
hidden in the many folds of my dress.
I've never felt such a feeling of calm,
I don't think I have ever loved you less.

How grateful I am for this masked ball-
for giving me the chance I need.
To my surprise I'm not nervous at all,
I am more than ready to do this deed.

I follow you silently into a room,
you smile at me, but do not recognise,
unaware that I am bringing your doom,
payback for the many year of lies

All too quickly the deed is done.
I laugh at how I am finally free.
I dispose of the knife, get ready to run-
I must be home when they come to tell me.

I am prepared, I'm ready with the lie,
I drag myself from my fake sickbed.
I clutch my heart and begin to cry
when they come to tell me my husband is dead.

Autumn Joys

There are simple things that fill me up with
happiness.
The endlessly grey days full of drizzle melting
into relentlessly stormy nights,
winds howling and trees shaking.
Their leaves already fragile,
turning from bright greens to deep rusty oranges
and browns,
collecting in piles,
waiting for children and adults alike to kick
them up and dance around as they fall again.
The heat of a bonfire on your face,
as your frozen fingers are warmed by hot
chocolates and mulled wines.
Fireworks that light up the sky and make
everything look
so wondrous and beautiful in the coloured lights.

Early winter sunrises,
leafless trees a stark contrast against a pale pink
skyline.
A fresh blanket of snow,
an artists canvas waiting to be rolled into
sculptures and thrown
at unsuspecting family members.

Walking through snow covered fields,
admiring your footprints behind you.
Hiding your cold ears and noses under thick hats
and scarves.
The coldness of your cheeks against the biting
wind.
Wrapping up in thick cardigans and warm wool
jumpers,
sitting under blankets in front of a roaring fire,
with hot cups of tea and well read books.
These are the simple things that fill my soul with
joy.

Our World Of Books

In our world,
We are children of Gods and daughters of siren
queens.
A red headed seer and a brown haired rebellion,
the angelic and demonic saving the world
together
as we hide from the other mother,
through the wardrobe and the looking glass.
There are giant peaches and scary teachers,
first wives and last unicorns.
We will sit on thrones of glass and iron swords
and
attend summer camps and specialist schools,
with Princes of Denmark and Kings of Scotland.
We will have our sword fights on cliff tops,
and visit secret gardens and mad tea parties.
Free dragons and ride broomsticks
with a boy who lived and a hero who is only
mostly dead.
From Baker Street via Kings Cross,
to Thornfield Hall and Manderley
through the districts and beyond the wall
from the shire towards Mordor
we will go to courts – of thorns and flames,
of kings and queens, of murderers and juries

we will catch fire and have dragons tattooed
And fall in love with a fallen star
there are star-crossed lovers and lovers who
have crossed the stars
perfectly imperfect marriages and brand new
romances
flat-shares and first kisses, true loves and true
losses.
In our world we have lived a thousand lives
and we will live a thousand more.

Bad Friends

Your smile is too big,
Your eyes are too cold,
Everything about you
screams scared of getting old.

We used to be so close
and its sad but its true,
now when you want cash
is when I hear from you.

We used to be friends,
I was totally a fan!
it all went downhill
when you married that man.

You say I'm your best friend,
your ride or die,
but its been a month now
and you haven't even said hi.

When did this happen?
You're judgmental and rude
and worst of all,
You've turned into a prude

I hate confrontation.
I don't want to fight,
but the way that you speak to me
it really isn't right

You're so self centred
I can't get a word in!
And constantly telling me
that you used to be thin.

You look down on my job,
my friends, my love life,
like you cant understand
I don't want to be a wife

Don't get me wrong
I'm glad that your happy,
but that doesn't mean that you
get to make me feel crappy!

It's getting to a point and
I cant decide which,
if you're really clueless
or if you're actually just a bitch.

Wilf

Sometimes the shadows creep in,
teasing at the corners of my mind so that I do not
notice
until I am overwhelmed.
Sometimes they are
all at once,
and I cannot fight
the barrage of anguish
as it consumes me.
I get so lost in the corners of my
mind—wandering and wandering in circles and
loops.
When my heart is sick and my soul feels cold
you show me what I am worth to you,
and warm me from the inside out.
You sit and wait for the tide to turn,
the ocean of emotions to recede and calm itself.
You do not try and force me from the dark.
You wrap me up in soft words and kind gestures,
like I wrap myself in knitted blankets.
Content to sit with me in the shadows,
a steady presence
to calm my
racing mind
until I am ready

to pull myself into the sun.
You are a light to combat the darkness,
an anchor that tethers me to this world
when the storms threaten to take me away.

I See You

I see your kind soul, your open heart,
especially when everything falls apart.
I see you look at the half empty cup
and how you will never, ever give up.

I see your strength, buried deep inside,
how hard you sometimes try to hide.
I see it when you are caused great pain,
when others use you for their own gain

I see your heart, In love, so light,
your happiness that shines so bright.
I see you make your own dreams come true
and I think how lucky, I am to have you.

I see when you're hurting, tears in your eyes.
when you are cut down by another set of lies.
I see you get up, ready to fight,
come out of the dark and into the light.

I see you clearly, I know this to be true.
Trust me, my love, I do see you.

Time Flies

You are so small and I am vast.
I am infinite, everlasting, absolute
keep running little one how long can you last.

I have seen all of the lives, all through the past.
I will see all the stories that come after you,
you are so small and I am vast

I cannot pass you by, no matter how much you
ask.
Sing for yourself and dance to your own tune,
keep running little one how long can you last.

I admire your passions, present and past,
you live a life so full, love however you choose.
You are so small and I am vast

You cannot keep hiding behind the mask,
there is only so long you can hold onto your
youth.
Keep running little one how long can you last

The time is coming, it's approaching fast,
no one can live forever, those are the rules.
You are so small and I am vast,
keep running little one how long can you last.

Bound

I have known you before.
I have known your cruelty and your kindness,
your passion and your promises.
I have known your love, your heart, body and
soul.
I have known you before and I will know you
again.
I will know you when our eyes meet for the first
time across a crowded room.
Something starts to bloom in my chest and I feel
a familiar pull in the deepest part of me.
You see into the very heart of me and somehow I
know.
You will take my hand, and the world will ignite.
You will always find me, and I will always know
you.
You would cross oceans to find me, and I would
know you if I was blind.
By the feel of your heartbeat and the sound of
your breathing.
When you stumble from this life into the next, I
will follow, as I always do.
We are bound to each others hearts, our souls
entangled for eternity.

You will always find me and I will always know you.
I have known you before this life, and I will know you in the next.

Not Enough Air

when you look at me
there isn't enough air in the room
time slows
and I can see every detail of you
the crinkle of your smile and the wrinkles
at the corner of your eyes
the curve of your wrists
and the shape of your hands
I know
when you kiss me
the world will stop
there will be no noise
but the beating of my own heart
trying to escape my chest
you will make the stars come out
and the sun go down
this feels like a moment
that people write about in songs
the fluttering in my heart and my stomach
feels like it will consume me
and I will get lost
in the colour of your eyes
and the smell of your skin
the world stops
and there isn't enough air in the room
when you look at me

Live For Yourself

Told from a young age we should have it all
together,
make the most of your looks they wont last
forever.
They want make-up that's 'barely there'
perfectly styled and well maintained hair.
We're told we're not pretty, we're round, too fat,
so we lose all the weight and now we're too flat?
We must dress well, fashion always on trend-
when does it actually ever end?
False nails, fake lashes, flawless skin,
we should be skinny but not too thin.

We should want a provider, but not dig for gold,
they'll trade us in anyway when we get too old.
They want us ambitious, career driven, rich,
but make sure you don't come across as a bitch.
Sinner, saint, virgin, whore,
"Maybe you should smile more"
Maybe you should be quiet and stick
to things you know, don't be such a prick.

I'm happy with my make up it makes me feel
fierce,

I don't care if you like it I'm gonna get
something pierced.
"Too many tattoos its ruined your skin"
My skin, my life, that you're not even in.
I like my tattoos, I got them for myself-
I didn't get ink to impress someone else.

They say friends but its kind of a lie,
we've all hung out with that 'nice guy'.
We really don't care what you have to say,
its still not gonna make us like you that way.
Unwanted opinions on pregnancy, hey-
when you get a uterus, then you get a say.
Go ahead throw a fit, tell me I look like a toad,
because my body is mine, not something you're
owed.

What's it gonna take for it to get through?
We live for ourselves, not for you.
We're told we can be anything,
but expected to be everything.
All these expectations make us feel crappy,
fuck the world just make yourself happy.

Fire & Ice

You are hard and full of ice, unmoving and
unyielding,
I am full of fire and heat, warm and open and
inviting.
You are strong and rigid, detached and distant,
I am flighty and frivolous, impetuous and
intense.

There is heat in your smile when you look at me;
the melting of ice and the warming of souls.
The heat is more bearable when your skin
touches mine,
calm contented embers replacing chaotic
wildfire.

Your serenity ebbs and flows around me, like a
cool stream on a warm day;
your tranquil indifference a stark contrast to my
suffocating intensity.
I am the fire that thaws your icy soul
and you keep me from being consumed by the
inferno within.

Your fuse ignites at a glacial pace, your cold
fury growing slowly

until it all is too much, and everything snaps
with the cold crack of ice breaking.
You throw your words with precision like
knives, cutting into every part of my soul
with your icy harshness.

I am full of passion and heat, anger rising
quickly and with force.
I am fire and wrath setting the world ablaze in a
haze of red mist and
I will show you my rage and you will be burned
by my pain.
shield your eyes and your soul before I scorch
and blacken both.

You detach yourself from the things I delight in,
sentimentality warring with cynicism.
Will you turn your coldness towards me?
will I singe you instead of keeping you warm?

Will you turn my heart to ice and make me too
bitter to love again.
Will I scar your soul with my rage and make you
forever unable to trust the heat.
We would burn and freeze too fast
until there's nothing left but ash and smoke.

The Earth Calls

No dancing with the devil, just dancing in the
dark.
The life in your veins is the song in your heart.
Sing to the stars and howl at the moon,
can you hear it calling you?

The brightest of stars in the blackest of nights,
walking through the forests in the pale
moonlight.
The leaves, they crackle and whisper too.
Can you hear it calling you?

The sweetest of raindrops falling on your face,
standing on the shore feeling the ocean sprays.
The calm gentle waves of a sea so blue,
can you hear it calling you?

The crack of lightning as it flashes through the
sky.
The deep rumble of thunder as it passes you by.
Does it make you feel refreshed, renewed?
Can you hear it calling you?

Put your hands in the soil, your toes in the sand.
Catch tiny snowflakes in the palm of your hand.

Take a deep breath, its long overdue,
can you hear it calling you?

Can you hear the earth calling your spirit home?

Good Energies

The stars whisper softly in the middle of the
night.
The moon, she guides you with her pale light.
She does not judge, but she sees all,
there are those who answer her call.

We come together and we come alone,
the maiden, mother and the crone.
Whispers in the day and spells at night,
some for the dark but most for the light.

There is no fear of stakes and pyres,
for no longer are we put to fires.
Sweep away the evil, burn a bit of sage,
the old ways live on, even in a new age.

Use good energy in all you do,
what you put out comes back to you.
Let the moon guide you with her pale light,
and the stars whisper to you in the middle of the
night.

A Watery Grave

I used to know a very old man,
he would tell me tales of the sea.
I try to remember all I can,
of the creatures there that should not be.

On a calm sea in the dead of night-
a sound is heard to make hearts race.
A song is sung so pure and light,
we have heard of what we face.

I send a prayer to the gods above.
Angels faces by the light of the moon.
Never will I see those that I love,
For I know that I have found my doom.

Her face is almost touching mine
and she smiles a feral smile at me.
I feel the shivers up my spine,
as she pulls me down into the sea.

I cannot fight the song nor waves.
I follow her down into my grave.

Over The Rainbow

The crimson sky as the sun rises,
violent streaks that bleed through a pink haze.
It speaks of deep romance for those we love
and remembrance for those we've lost.

The sun sinks in an amber glow,
soft and warm like the embers of a fire.
It is pumpkins and campfires,
and spreads comfort and warmth.

When it hangs high in all its glory,
the sun is golden, shining over
bright daffodils and buttercups
sunflowers stand tall towards it.

the colours of the leaves on the trees,
different shades and hues.
The mossy blanket on a forest floor
and the fresh beauty of verdant hillsides.

White wispy clouds against azure skies.
Small boats floating lazily on cerulean seas.
A calmness and serenity,
as I gaze towards the horizon.

A blanket of stars starts to shine
against an indigo sky,
between dusk and twilight
it feels like fairies and magic.

The beautiful bright colours of wild flowers,
violets and lavenders,
rolling fields of heather and saffron
to please the mind and soul

A spectrum of colours and textures
that this universe has created.
The beauty and hope in nature
fills all the world with joy.

Heavenly Bodies

1
Look up at the stars
as they keep their twilight watch
and think how lucky.

2
Bask in the moonlight,
keep good counsel with the stars
you may need their help.

3
Walk barefoot through night,
and sing softly to the stars.
Come, howl at the moon.

Milton Keynes UK
Ingram Content Group UK Ltd.
UKHW020938220424
441551UK00019B/1432

9 789358 316384